On
Translation

'One of the most distinguished and prolific philosophers of his generation.'
The Daily Telegraph

Praise for the series

'. . . allows a space for distinguished thinkers to write about their
passions.'
The Philosophers' Magazine

'. . . deserve high praise.'
Boyd Tonkin, The Independent (UK)

'This is clearly an important series. I look forward to receiving
future volumes.'
Frank Kermode, author of Shakespeare's Language

'. . . both rigorous and accessible.'
Humanist News

'. . . the series looks superb.'
Quentin Skinner

'. . . an excellent and beautiful series.'
Ben Rogers, author of A.J. Ayer: A Life

'Routledge's *Thinking in Action* series is the theory junkie's
answer to the eminently pocketable Penguin 60s series.'
Mute Magazine (UK)

'Routledge's new series, *Thinking in Action*, brings philosophers
to our aid . . .'
The Evening Standard (UK)

'. . . a welcome series by Routledge.'
Bulletin of Science, Technology and Society (Can)

'Routledge's innovative new *Thinking in Action* series takes the
concept of philosophy a step further.'
The Bookwatch

PAUL RICOEUR

Translated by Eileen Brennan

With an introduction by
Richard Kearney

On Translation

Routledge
Taylor & Francis Group
LONDON AND NEW YORK

First published in 2004 in French as 'Sur la
traduction' by Bayard, 3 et 5 rue Bayard, 75008 Paris,
France

English translation as 'On Translation' first published 2006
by Routledge
2 Park Square, Milton Park, Abingdon, Oxon OX14 4RN

Simultaneously published in the USA and Canada
by Routledge
270 Madison Ave, New York, NY 10016

Routledge is an imprint of the Taylor & Francis Group, an informa business

Typeset in Joanna MT and DIN by
RefineCatch Ltd, Bungay, Suffolk
Printed and bound in Great Britain by
TJ International Ltd, Padstow, Cornwall

British Library Cataloguing in Publication Data
A catalogue record for this book is available from the British Library

Library of Congress Cataloging-in-Publication Data
Ricoeur, Paul.
  [sur la traduction. English]
  On translation / Paul Ricoeur; translated by Eileen Brennan, with an introduction by
Richard Kearney
    p. cm. — (Thinking in action)
  1. Translating and interpreting.   I. Title.   II. Series.
P306.R53713 2006
418'.02—dc22   2005001403

ISBN10: 0–415–35777–2 (hbk)
ISBN10: 0–415–35778–0 (pbk)
ISBN10: 0–203–00383–7 (ebk)

ISBN13: 978–0–415–35777–7 (hbk)
ISBN13: 978–0–415–35778–4 (pbk)
ISBN13: 978–0–203–00383–1 (ebk)

Note on the texts

The three essays in this volume were published together in French by Bayard, Paris in 2004 under the title *Sur la traduction*. 'Translation as challenge and source of happiness' was originally the text of an address given at the German Historical Institute of Paris on 15 April 1997; 'The paradigm of translation' (inaugural lecture at the Faculty of Protestant Theology, Paris, in October 1998) was first published in *Esprit* 853 (June 1999). 'A "Passage" ' first appeared in *Sur la traduction*.

Introduction: Ricoeur's philosophy of translation

Richard Kearney

Translation has been a central feature of Paul Ricoeur's philosophy, though it was not until his later years that he actually made it an explicit theme of his work. The three essays collected in this volume are three such instances.

Well before Ricoeur thematized the subject, the act of translation was something which this leading twentieth-century thinker actually *performed* in his philosophical practice. Ricoeur was an inveterate mediator, someone who navigated and negotiated transits between rival intellectual positions. He was unequalled as a diplomat of philosophical exchange, forever finding a point of commerce – if not always resolution – between ostensibly irreconcilable viewpoints. Between Continental and Anglo-Saxon thought at the most general level. Then, within the Continental tradition more specifically, between existentialism and structuralism; between hermeneutics and Critical Theory; between phenomenology and the human sciences; between Freudian psychoanalysis and Hegelian dialectics; between literary theory and the philosophy of religion; between historical understanding (*Verstehen*) and scientific explanation (*Erklären*); between psychology and neuroscience; between ethics and politics, and so on. What is remarkable in all these critical intercessions is that Ricoeur never ceased to respect both adversarial partners in the exchange, deftly transmuting conflict into conversation. And this without ever sacrificing depth of conviction or acuity of evaluation. In his philosophical role as translator, Ricoeur was, I believe, unrivalled in his time. In a sense, one could say that Ricoeur's thought represented both philosophy *as* translation and a philosophy *of* translation.

Before proceeding to a more detailed account of Ricoeur's thematic analysis of translation, however, I wish to offer a brief overview of Ricoeur's expansive intellectual itinerary from his youthful explorations of existential phenomenology to his final writings on narrative, memory and history.

RICOEUR'S INTELLECTUAL ITINERARY

Paul Ricoeur died in his sleep at the age of ninety-two at his home in Châtenay-Malabry (Hauts-de-Seine outside Paris) on 20 May 2005.

Ricoeur was one of the most challenging, hospitable and enduring thinkers of the twentieth century. Born in Valence, France, in 1913, he taught as professor of philosophy at the universities of Strasbourg, Paris (IV and X) and Louvain and as John Niveen Chair at the University of Chicago. Ricoeur published over thirty major works during his lifetime, ranging from existentialism and phenomenology to psychoanalysis, politics, religion and the theory of language. But Ricoeur was much more than a brilliant intellectual mediator between competing schools of thought. He also, and most significantly, developed his own particular brand of philosophical hermeneutics. Determined to find a path between (1) the romantic hermeneutics of Schleiermacher and Gadamer and (2) the more radical hermeneutics of deconstruction (Derrida, Caputo) and Critical Theory (Habermas), Ricoeur endeavoured to chart a middle way which combined both the empathy and conviction of the former and the suspicion and detachment of the latter. He himself never gave a name to this third path (he was wary of founding a new ideology or -ism). But I think we would not be far wrong in naming it dialogical or diacritical hermeneutics. There were not many major figures in contemporary thought – Husserl, Freud, Rawls, Heidegger, Wittgenstein, Foucault, Lévi-Strauss, Saussure, Austen, Arendt, Jaspers, Marcel, Habermas, Levinas, Derrida – with whom he did not engage in robust debate.

Taking his tune from such German hermeneutic thinkers as Dilthey, Heidegger and Gadamer, Ricoeur elaborated a complex set of inquiries into what he called the enigma of 'semantic innovation'. How does new meaning come to be? How do we reconfigure the meanings of the past? These basic hermeneutic questions were guided by the thesis that existence is itself a mode of interpretation (*hermeneia*). Or, as the hermeneutic maxim went: *Life interprets itself*. But where Heidegger concentrated directly on a fundamental ontology of interpretation, Ricoeur advanced what he called the 'long route' of multiple hermeneutic detours. This brought him into dialogue with the human sciences where philosophy discovers its limits in what is outside of philosophy. It prompted him to invigilate those border exchanges where meaning traverses the various signs and disciplines in which being is interpreted by human understanding. Ricoeur thus challenged Heidegger's view that Being is accessible through the 'short route' of human existence (*Dasein*) which understands itself through its own possibilities. He argued instead that the meaning of Being is always mediated through an endless process of interpretations – cultural, religious, political, historical and scientific. Hence Ricoeur's basic definition of hermeneutics as the 'art of deciphering indirect meaning'.

Philosophy, for Ricoeur, was hermeneutical to the extent that it read hidden meanings in apparent meanings. And the task of hermeneutics was to show how existence arrives at expression, and later again at reflection, through the perpetual exploration of the significations that emerge in the symbolic works of culture. More particularly, human existence only becomes a self by retrieving meanings which first reside 'outside' of itself in the social institutions and cultural monuments in which the life of the spirit is inscribed.

One of the first critical targets of Ricoeur's hermeneutics was the idealist doctrine that the self is transparent to itself. In two of his earliest works — The Voluntary and the Involuntary (1950) and The Symbolism of Evil (1960) — Ricoeur exploded the pretensions of the cogito to be self-founding and self-knowing. He insisted that the shortest route from self to self is through the other. Or to put it in Ricoeur's felicitous formula: 'to say self is not to say I'. Why? Because the hermeneutic self is much more than an autonomous subject. Challenging the reign of the transcendental ego, Ricoeur proposed the notion of oneself-as-another in an influential work which carried this same title (1990 in French; 1992 in English). Here he spoke of a soi that passes beyond the illusory confines of the moi and discovers its meaning in and through the linguistic mediations of signs and symbols, stories and ideologies, metaphors and myths. In the most positive hermeneutic scenario, outlined in his three-volume Time and Narrative in the eighties, the self returns to itself after numerous hermeneutic detours through the languages of others, to find itself enlarged and enriched by the odyssey. The Cartesian model of the cogito as 'master and possessor' of meaning is henceforth radically subverted.

We thus find Ricoeur steering a medial course beyond the rationalism of Descartes and Kant, on the one hand, and the phenomenology of Husserl, Heidegger and existentialists, on the other. (Ricoeur actually began a translation of Husserl's *Ideas* during his captivity in a German prisoner-of-war camp in the early 1940s which was published in 1950.) Where Husserl located meaning in the subject's intuition of the 'things themselves' as manifest in transcendental consciousness, Ricoeur followed the hermeneutic dictum that intuition is always a matter of interpretation. This implied that things are always given to us *indirectly* through a detour of signs; but it did not entail an embrace of existentialist irrationalism. The interpretation (*hermeneia*) of indirect or tacit meaning invites us to think *more*, not to abandon speculative thought altogether. And nowhere was this more evident than in the challenge posed by symbolic meaning (Ricoeur's first explicitly hermeneutic work was entitled *The Symbolism of Evil*, published in 1960). By symbols Ricoeur understood all expressions of double meaning wherein a primary meaning referred beyond itself to a second meaning which is never given immediately. This 'surplus meaning' provokes interpretation. *The symbol gives rise to thought*, as Ricoeur put it in what was to be become his most celebrated maxim.

Let me add, at his point, a personal note. An obituary memory as it were. Every time I visited Ricoeur over the years at his home in Châtenay-Malabry, outside Paris, I was invariably struck by the hosts of owls furnishing his bureau and library. Ricoeur was, in more ways than one, the living epitome of the Owl of Minerva — a thinker who always preferred the long route over the short cut and never wrote an essay or book until he had first experienced and questioned deeply what it was he was writing about. He, like the Owl of Wisdom in Hegel's legendary example, only took flight at dusk when he had fully attended to what transpired (in the realm of both action and suffering) during the long day's journey into night. The fact that Ricoeur endured for almost a century – following in the footsteps of his fellow hermeneutician, Gadamer (is there something in the hermeneutic water?) – additionally qualified him, of course, for the emblematic title of a wise old owl. Someone born in 1913 who witnessed three world wars (counting the Cold War), suffered years of prison captivity under the Nazis, taught in dozens of universities throughout the world and published several dozen major volumes of philosophy, knows, I think, what he is talking about when he completes a book in his ninetieth year entitled *La mémoire, l'histoire, l'oubli*. It is a privilege, I would suggest, for us, his readers, to learn deeply from his lived reflections.

Some time before he died Ricoeur received a gift of a marzipan owl statue. He placed it by his bed and gleefully planned to play a joke on his grandchildren (whom he called affectionately 'les petits becs'). During their next visit he was going to pretend he was biting into one of the many marble owls in his collection, as if this had become one of his daily culinary habits! He didn't live to carry out the joke. But it is a telling token of Ricoeur's mischievous sense of humour and love of life.

RICOEUR'S PHILOSOPHY OF TRANSLATION

There are two paradigms of translation for Ricoeur. There is, first, the *linguistic paradigm* which refers to how words relate to meanings within language or between languages. And there is, second, the *ontological paradigm* which refers to how translation occurs between one human self and another.[1] Let me say something about each.

Language is one yet languages are many. In this very distinction lies the primordial need for translation. What all languages share in common is a capacity to mediate between a human speaker and a world of meanings (actual and possible) spoken about. But if this function constitutes the unifying property of language, the fact there there exist a plurality of languages, both living and dead, means that we are faced with a double duty of translation, internal and external.

A brief look at the historical development of the philosophy of translation will help clarify the issue. Some of the earliest reflections on the problems and enigmas of translation go back, at least in Western history, to the great encounters between cultures. In classical times, we find the translation between Greek and Latin languages to be a crucial landmark; while the famous feats of biblical translation from Hebrew and Aramaic to Greek and Latin, ranging from the Septuagint to the decisive translations of St Jerome (author of the Vulgate), or later again, of Luther in German, or the King James authors in English, mark yet another set of milestones in the history of interlinguistic translation. Among the earliest words for a translator were in Greek *hermeneus* and in Latin *interpres*. Both terms carry the sense of an intermediary labouring between two distinct languages or speakers. The term translator, as we know it today, arises from the Latin verb *transfero, transfere, translatum*, which evolves into the term *translatare, translater* in the Romance languages of the Middle Ages (hence the later English *translate*). In the fifteenth century, the Italian humanist Leonardo Bruni became the first modern thinker to devote an entire scientific treatise to the art of translation, entitled *De Interpretatione Recta* (1420). Here we witness the original appearance of the term *traducere* referring to a unitary concept of translation, and giving rise in the sixteenth century to the French term *traducteur*, employed by the human- ist Etienne Doler.[2] The twentieth century saw a number of influential theorists of translation, from Croce and Rosenz- weig to Benjamin (*The Task of the Translator*) and Steiner (*After Babel*). The present volume of essays by Ricoeur, appearing as it does at the beginning of the twenty-first century (the ori- ginal French edition, *Sur la traduction*, was published in 2004), follows firmly and faithfully in the footsteps of these intel- lectual predecessors. What Ricoeur adds is a singularly her- meneutic twist, which I touch on below.

There is no doubt that some of the great translations of biblical and classical texts played formative roles in the devel- opment of both national and cultural identities. One thinks of the huge influence exerted by Luther's German translation of the Bible, or the Moravian Brethren's Czech translation, or the Genevan French translation; not to mention the crucial role played by renditions of classical texts in the birth of the Renaissance, the Enlightenment or Romanticism. In all these instances, the transmigration of one linguistic thesaurus into another was linked with modern ideas of human emancipa- tion and change. And the momentous encounter with the Other outside the nation, or indeed the European world gen- erally – with the discovery of other continents and civiliza- tions from the fifteenth century onwards – was a crucial reminder of the necessity of translation. Thus understood, translation has always been, in Antoine Berman's resonant phrase, *une épreuve de l'étranger*.[3] For better or for worse.

Translation can be understood here in both a specific and a general sense. In the specific sense – the one in common contemporary usage – it signals the work of translating the meanings of one particular language into another. In the more generic sense, it indicates the everyday act of speaking as a way not only of translating oneself to oneself (inner to outer, private to public, unconscious to conscious, etc.) but also and more explicitly of translating oneself to others. As Dominico Jervolino puts it:

> To speak is already to translate (even when one is speaking one's own native language or when one is speaking to oneself); further, one has to take into account the plurality of languages, which demand a more exacting encounter with the different Other. One is tempted to say that there is a plurality of languages because we are originally plural. The encounter with the Other cannot be avoided. If one accepts the necessary nature of the encounter, linguistic pluralism appears no longer as a malediction, as the received interpretation of the myth of Babel would have it, but as a condition which requires us to surrender the all-encompassing dream of a perfect language (and of a global translation, so to speak, without residues). The partiality and the finitude of individual languages is then viewed not as an insurmountable obstacle but as the very precondition of communication among individuals.[4]

Jervolino is explicating here one of Ricoeur's most central insights. Ricoeur compares the work of the translator to that of a middleman between 'two masters', between an author and a reader, a self and another. He underlines the word 'work', stressing the importance of a labour both of memory and of mourning. As such, he borrows liberally from Freud's famous notion of 'working through' (*Durcharbeitung*). This emphasis on the *labour* character of translation refers to the common experience of tension and suffering which the translator undergoes as he/she checks the impulse to reduce the otherness of the other, thereby subsuming alien meaning into one's own scheme of things. The work of translation might thus be said to carry a double duty: to expropriate oneself as one appropriates the other. We are called to make our language put on the stranger's clothes at the same time as we invite the stranger to step into the fabric of our own speech.

Ricoeur argues that good translations involve some element of openness to the other. Indeed he suggests that we be prepared to forfeit our native language's claim to self-sufficiency – which can sometimes go to extremes of nationalism and chauvinism – in order to 'host' (qua *hospes*) the 'foreign' (*hostis*). Indeed, as the linguist Émile Benveniste points out in *Le vocabulaire des institutions indo-européennes*, the two terms *hospes* and *hostis* are etymologically akin.[5] Following Benveniste, Ricoeur writes:

> Despite the conflictual character which renders the task of the translator dramatic, he or she will find satisfaction in what I would like to call *linguistic hospitality*. Its predicament is that of a correspondence without complete adhesion. This is a fragile condition, which admits of no verification other than a new translation . . . a sort of duplication of the work of the translator which is possible in virtue of a minimum of bilingualism: to translate afresh after the translator.

And he adds:

> Just as in a narration it is always possible to tell the story in a different way, likewise in translation it is always possible to translate otherwise, without ever hoping to bridge the gap between equivalence and perfect adhesion. Linguistic hospitality, therefore, is the act of inhabiting the word of the Other paralleled by the act of receiving the word of the Other into one's own home, one's own dwelling.[6]

Linguistic hospitality calls us to forgo the lure of omnipotence: the illusion of a total translation which would provide a perfect replica of the original. Instead it asks us to respect the fact that the semantic and syntactic fields of two languages are not the same, or exactly reducible the one to the other. Connotations, contexts and cultural characteristics will always exceed any slide rule of neat equations between tongues. Short of some kind of abstract symbolic logic or fantasy Esperanto logos there is no single unitary language. Translation is always *after Babel*. It is forever compelled to acknowledge the finite limits of language, the multiplicity of different tongues. To function authentically, therefore, the translator must renounce the dream of a return to some adamantine logos of pure correspondences. The attempt to retrieve a prelapsarian paradise of timeless signs is futile. Even the Enlightenment ideal of a perfect universal language was obliged to recognize the genuine resistances of cultural differences predicated upon linguistic diversities. Indeed, most attempts to instantiate an absolute universal language proved, in point of fact, to be thinly disguised imperial ploys to impose one particular language (French, English, Spanish, etc.) over other politically subordinate ones.

As soon as there is language there is interpretation, that is translation. *In principio fuit interpres*. Words exist in time and space, and thus have a history of meanings which alter and evolve. All translation involves some aspect of dialogue between self and stranger. Dialogue means just that, *dia-legein*, welcoming the difference. It is for this reason that in his essay 'The paradigm of translation' Ricoeur proposes translation as a model of hermeneutics. Both in its normal role as a transfer of meaning from one language to another and in its more specific role as a transfer of understanding between different members of the same linguistic community, translation entails an exposure to strangeness. We are dealing with both an alterity residing outside the home language *and* an alterity residing within it.

> The gap between a hypothetical perfect language and the concreteness of a living language is felt again and again in the linguistic exchange: it is always possible to say the same thing in a different way. Now, to say something in a different way, to say it in other terms, is exactly what a translator does from one language to the other. The inputs at the two ends, the two halves of the problem, so to speak, clarify each other and present again the enigma and the richness of the relationship with the Other.[7]

It might be noted that Ricoeur's theory of translation here follows a similar emphasis to his theory of the text as model of interpretation in the seventies and eighties. In both cases, Ricoeur underlines the 'distancing' of sense. In the case of the written text this refers to how meaning gains autonomy from (1) the intention of the original author, (2) the original world of circumstances in which the author wrote or which s/he wrote about, and (3) the original readers of the text when it was first produced (e.g. the Greek community who read Homer's *Odyssey*). A similar aspect of 'distantiation' occurs in translation where the estrangement of meaning precedes and even provokes the subsequent act of reading as a renewed reappropriation of the original meaning. Or as Ricoeur liked to put it, the best path to selfhood is through otherness. Thus while Schleiermacher, Gadamer and the romantic hermeneuts tended to favour a somewhat Platonic model of dialogue as a return to original meanings, Ricoeur might be said to favour a more Aristotelian model which stresses a plurality of meanings and a methodical appreciation of the complex 'poetics' and 'rhetorics' involved in the interpretation of linguistic meaning. (Hence, as already noted, the importance of Ricoeur's call, *pace* Gadamer and Heidegger, for a rigorous critical relationship with the human sciences – including linguistics – and a surpassing of the old dichotomy between 'understanding' and 'explanation'.) For Ricoeur the matter is clear: there is no self-understanding possible without the labour of mediation through signs, symbols, narratives and texts. The idealist romantic self, sovereign master of itself and all it surveys, is replaced by an engaged self which only finds itself after it has traversed the field of foreignness and returned to itself again, this time altered and enlarged, 'othered'. The *moi* gives way to the *soi*, or more precisely to *soi-même comme un autre*. The arc of translation epitomizes this journey from self through the other, reminding us of the irreducible finitude and contingency of all language.

For Ricoeur, the task of outer translation finds echoes in the work of inner translation. Indeed the very problem of human identity, as he shows in *Oneself as Another*, involves a discovery of an other within the very depths of the self. This other within is itself plural, signifying by turns the unconscious, the body, the call of conscience, the traces of our relations with other human beings, or the sign of transcendence inscribed in the deepest interiority of the human heart. This means that the question of human identity, or more exactly the answer to the question '*who* are you?', always entails a translation between the self and others both within the self and outside the self. Every subject, as Ricoeur puts it, is a tapestry of stories heard and told. This makes of each one of us a narrative identity, operating as both authors and readers of our own lives. Which is another way of saying, *translators of* our own lives. Life stories and life histories are always parts of larger stories and histories in which we find ourselves interwoven or entwined (*empêtré*). This is where the paradigm of translation as transference to and fro, forward and backward, reveals its everyday power. 'To think, to speak is always to translate, even when one speaks to oneself, when one discovers the traces (and one cannot subsist without them) of the Other in oneself. After all language, understood as a peculiarly human attribute, is always coupled to a specific and particular language and to the variety and plurality of languages'.[8] Indeed, Ricoeur goes so far as to suggest that the future ethos of European politics, and eventually of world politics, should be one based upon an exchange of memories and narratives between different nations, for it is only when we translate our own wounds into the language of strangers and retranslate the wounds of strangers into our own language that healing and reconciliation can take place.

This is ultimately what Ricoeur intends when he describes the ethics of translation as an interlinguistic hospitality. The world is made up of a plurality of human beings, cultures, tongues. Humanity exists in the plural mode. Which means that any legitimate form of universality must always – if the hermeneutic model of translation is observed – find its equivalent plurality. The creative tension between the universal and the plural ensures that the task of translation is an endless one, a work of tireless memory and mourning, of appropriation and disappropriation, of taking up and letting go, of expressing oneself and welcoming others. The final word of Ricoeur's last major published book, *Memory, History and Forgetting*, is 'incompletion' (*inachèvement*).[9] And this is telling. For it acknowledges that translation, understood as an endlessly unfinished business, is a signal not of failure but of hope.

On Translation
Paul Ricoeur

One

You will allow me to express my gratitude to the DVA Foundation[1] in Stuttgart for inviting me to be one of the contributors at the presentation of the 1996 Franco-German Translation Prize. You agreed that I give the title 'Translation as challenge and source of happiness' to these few remarks.

Indeed, I would like to place my remarks, dedicated to translation's great difficulties and small delights, under the aegis of the title *The Test of the Foreign*,[2] which the late lamented Antoine Berman gave to his remarkable essay subtitled *Culture and Translation in Romantic Germany*.

First and at greater length, I will speak about the difficulties linked to translation as a wager, easier said than done and occasionally impossible to take up. These difficulties are accurately summarized in the term 'test' [*épreuve*], in the double sense of 'ordeal' [*peine endurée*] and 'probation': testing period, as we say, of a plan, of a desire or perhaps even of an urge, the urge to translate.

To throw light on this test, I suggest comparing the 'translator's task', which Walter Benjamin speaks about, with 'work' in the double sense that Freud gives to that word when, in one essay, he speaks of the 'work of remembering' and, in another essay, he speaks of the 'work of mourning'. In translation too, work is advanced with some salvaging and some acceptance of loss.

Salvaging of what? Loss of what? That is the question that the term 'foreign' poses in Berman's title. In reality, two partners are connected through the act of translating, the foreign – a term that covers the work, the author, his language – and the reader, recipient of the translated work. And, between the two, the translator who passes on the whole message, who has it go from one idiom to another. It is in this uncomfortable position of mediator that the test in question lies. Franz Rosenzweig gave this test the form of a paradox. To translate, he says, is to serve two masters: the foreigner with his work, the reader with his desire for appropriation, foreign author, reader dwelling in the same language as the translator. Indeed, this paradox falls within the domain of an unparalleled problematic, doubly sanctioned by a vow of faithfulness and a suspicion of betrayal. Schleiermacher, whom one of our prize-winners honours this evening, broke the paradox up into two phrases: 'bringing the reader to the author', 'bringing the author to the reader'.

It is in this exchange, in this chiasmus that the equivalent of what we have already called the work of remembering, the work of mourning, lies. The work of remembering first: this work, which one can also liken to a parturition, is concerned with the two poles of translation. In one way, it attacks the view that the mother tongue is sacred, the mother tongue's nervousness around its identity.

This resistance on the side of the reader must not be underestimated. The pretensions to self-sufficiency, the refusal to allow the foreign mediate, have secretly nourished numerous linguistic ethnocentrisms, and more seriously, numerous pretensions to the same cultural hegemony that we have been able to observe in relation to Latin, from late antiquity to the end of the Middle Ages and even beyond the Renaissance, in relation to French in the classical era, and in relation to English today. I have used the psychoanalytic term 'resistance' to convey the sense of this deceitful refusal to have the language of reception subjected to the test of the foreign.

But the resistance to the work of translation, as an equivalent of the work of remembering, is not weaker on the side of the foreign language. The translator meets with this resistance at numerous stages of his enterprise. He encounters it, at a very early stage, as the presumption of non-translatability, which inhibits him even before he tackles the work. Everything transpires as though in the initial fright, in what is sometimes the anguish of beginning, the foreign text towers up like a lifeless block of resistance to translation. To some extent, this initial presumption is only a fantasy nourished by the banal admission that the original will not be duplicated by another original; an admission that I call banal, because it resembles that of every collector facing the best reproduction of a work of art. He knows about the most serious flaw, i.e. not being the original. But a fantasy of perfect translation takes over from this banal dream of the duplicated original. It reaches a peak in the fear that, being translation, the translation will only be bad translation, by definition as it were.

But the resistance to translation takes on a less fantastical form once the work of translation begins. The segments of untranslatability are scattered through the text, making the translation a drama, and the wish for a good translation a wager. In this respect, the translation of poetic works is the one which has exercised minds the most, to be precise, in the age of German Romanticism, from Herder to Goethe, from Schiller to Novalis, then later still in von Humboldt and Schleiermacher, and up to today, in Benjamin and Rosenzweig.

Indeed, poetry presented the serious difficulty of the inseparable combination of sense and sonority, of the signified and the signifier. But the translation of philosophical works, which is of greater concern to us today, reveals difficulties of a different and, in a sense, also inflexible nature, insofar as it springs up at the actual level of the carving up of semantic fields, which turn out to be not strictly superimposable on one another. And the difficulty is at its height with the primary words, the *Grundwörter*, which the translator sometimes wrongly makes it a rule to translate word for word, the same word receiving a fixed equivalent in the target language. But this legitimate constraint has its limits, insofar as these great primary words, *Vorstellung, Aufhebung, Dasein, Ereignis*, are themselves summaries of long textuality where whole contexts are mirrored, to say nothing of the phenomena of intertextuality concealed in the actual stamp [*la frappe*] of the word. Intertextuality which is sometimes equivalent to revival, transformation, refutation of earlier uses by authors who fall within the same tradition of thought or opposing traditions.

Not only are the semantic fields not superimposed on one another, but the syntaxes are not equivalent, the turns of phrase do not serve as a vehicle for the same cultural legacies; and what is to be said about the half-silent connotations, which alter the best-defined denotations of the original vocabulary, and which drift, as it were, between the signs, the sentences, the sequences whether short or long. It is to this heterogeneity that the foreign text owes its resistance to translation and, in this sense, its intermittent untranslatability.

As regards philosophical texts, furnished with a rigorous semantics, the paradox of translation is exposed. Thus, the logician Quine, in the field of English language's analytic philosophy, considers a non-adequate correspondence between two texts to be an absurd idea. The dilemma is the following: in a good translation, the two texts, source and target, must be matched with one another through a third non-existent text. Indeed, the problem is saying the same thing or claiming to say the same thing in two different ways. But this same thing, this identical meaning is not given anywhere in the manner of a third text, whose status would be that of the third man in Plato's *Parmenides*, a third party between the idea of man and the human examples that are thought to participate in the real and true idea. In the absence of this third text, where the actual meaning would lie, the semantic original, there is only one recourse, i.e. the critical reading of a few, if not polyglot then at least bilingual, specialists, critical reading equivalent to a private retranslation, where our capable reader redoes the work of translation, for his own purposes, taking on, in turn, the test of translation and meeting with the same paradox of an equivalence without adequacy.

I will now open parentheses. Talking about retranslation by the reader, I am broaching the more general problem of the ceaseless retranslation of the main works, the great classics of global culture, the Bible, Shakespeare, Dante, Cervantes, Molière. It should perhaps even be said that it is in retranslation that we most clearly observe the urge to translate, stimulated by the dissatisfaction with regard to existing translations. I am closing these parentheses again.

We have followed the translator ever since the anguish that kept him from beginning, through his struggle with the text, which has characterized the whole of his work; we leave him where the finished work leaves him, i.e. in a dissatisfied state.

Antoine Berman, much of whose work I have thus reread on this occasion, uses a happy turn of phrase to summarize the two forms of resistance: that of the text to be translated and that of the translation's language of reception. I quote: 'On the psychological level', he says, 'the translator is ambivalent. He wants to force the two sides, force his language so that it is filled with incongruity, force the other language so that it is interned [*se dé-porter*] in his mother tongue.'

Our comparison with the work of remembering, mentioned by Freud, has thus found its proper equivalent in the work of translation, work won on the two fronts of a two-part resistance. Well, at this stage of the dramatization it happens that the work of mourning finds its equivalent in translation studies and puts its harsh but invaluable corrective into it. I will summarize it in one line: give up the ideal of the perfect translation. This renunciation alone makes it possible to live, as agreed deficiency, the impossibility, articulated a short while ago, of serving two masters: the author and the reader. This mourning also makes it possible to take on the two supposedly conflicting tasks of 'bringing the author to the reader' and 'bringing the reader to the author'. In brief, the courage to take on the well-known problem of faithfulness and betrayal: vow/suspicion. But with which perfect translation is this renunciation, this work of mourning, concerned? Lacoue-Labarthe and Jean-Luc Nancy provided a really good account of it in the German Romantics under the heading, 'the literary absolute'.

This absolute governs an approximation enterprise, which has taken different names, 'regeneration' of the target language in Goethe, 'potentiating' the source language in Novalis, convergence of the two-part process of *Bildung* with work on both sides in von Humboldt.

Now this dream has not been entirely misleading insofar as it has encouraged the ambition of revealing the hidden face of the source language of the work to be translated and, *vice versa*, the ambition of de-provincialising the mother tongue, which is invited to think of itself as one language amongst others, ultimately to see itself as foreign. But this desire for perfect translation has taken on other forms. I will cite only two of them: first the cosmo-political design in the wake of the *Aufklärung*, the dream of building up the complete library, which would be, by accumulation, the Book, the infinitely ramified network of the translations of all the works in all the languages, crystallizing into a sort of universal library from which the untranslatabilities would all have been erased. According to this dream, which would also be that of a rationality fully released from cultural constraints and community restrictions, this dream of omni-translation would try to fill the interlinguistic space of communication and make good the lack of universal language. The other aspiration of perfect translation was embodied in messianic expectation, which Walter Benjamin revived at the level of language in that magnificent text, *The Translator's Task*. What would then be aspired to would be the pure language, as Benjamin puts it, that every translation carries within itself as its messianic echo. In all these forms, the dream of the perfect translation amounts to the wish that translation would gain, gain without losing. It is this very same gain without loss that we must mourn until we reach an acceptance of the impassable difference of the peculiar and the foreign. Recaptured universality would try to abolish the memory of the foreign and maybe the love of one's own language, hating the mother tongue's provincialism. Erasing its own history, the same universality would turn all who are foreign to it into language's stateless persons, exiles who would have given up the search for the asylum afforded by a language of reception. In brief, errant nomads.

And it is this mourning for the absolute translation that produces the happiness associated with translating. The happiness associated with translating is a gain when, tied to the loss of the linguistic absolute, it acknowledges the difference between adequacy and equivalence, equivalence without adequacy. There is its happiness. When the translator acknowledges and assumes the irreducibility of the pair, the peculiar and the foreign, he finds his reward in the recognition of the impassable status of the dialogicality of the act of translating as the reasonable horizon of the desire to translate. In spite of the agonistics that make a drama of the translator's task, he can find his happiness in what I would like to call *linguistic hospitality*.

So its scheme is definitely that of a correspondence without adequacy. Fragile condition which accepts, in place of verification, only that work of retranslation, which I mentioned a short while ago, understood as a sort of exercise in doubling the work of the translator through minimum bilingualism: retranslate after the translator. I took these two models, more or less comparable to the psychoanalysis of the work of memory and of the work of mourning, as my starting point, but I did so in order to say that, just as in the act of telling a story, we can translate differently, without hope of filling the gap between equivalence and total adequacy. Linguistic hospitality, then, where the pleasure of dwelling in the other's language is balanced by the pleasure of receiving the foreign word at home, in one's own welcoming house.

Two

There are two access routes to the problem posed by the act of translating: either take the term 'translation' in the strict sense of the transfer of a spoken message from one language to another or take it in the broad sense as synonymous with the interpretation of any meaningful whole within the same speech community.

Both approaches are legitimate: the first, chosen by Antoine Berman in *The Test of the Foreign*, takes account of the solid fact of the plurality and the diversity of languages; the second, followed by George Steiner in *After Babel*,[1] is directed at the combining phenomenon, which the author summarizes in this way: 'To understand is to translate.' I have chosen to start from the first, which allows the relationship of the peculiar to the foreign to pass into the foreground, and in this way I will lead you to the second under the direction of the difficulties and the paradoxes created by translation from one language to another.

So let us start out from the plurality and the diversity of languages, and let us note down a first fact: it is because men speak different languages that there is translation. This fact is that of the *diversity of languages*, to go back to Wilhelm von Humboldt's title. Now, this fact is simultaneously an enigma: why not a single language, and above all why so many languages, five or six thousand according to the ethnologists? Every Darwinian measure of usefulness and adaptation in the struggle for survival is routed out; this multiplicity, impossible to count, is not only useless, but is also harmful. Indeed, if the intracommunity exchange is ensured by each language's power of integration taken separately, the exchange with what is outside the linguistic community is ultimately rendered impracticable owing to what Steiner calls 'a harmful prodigality'. But what makes it enigmatic is not only the jamming of communication (the myth of Babel, which we are going to say more about, calls it 'scattering' on the geographic plane and 'confounding' on the communication plane); it is also the contrast with some other features which also have to do with language. First, the well-known fact of the universality of language: 'All men speak'; that is a measure of humanity alongside the tool, the institution, burial; by language, let us understand the use of signs, which are not things, but concern things[2] – the exchange of signs in interlocution: the main role of a common language at the level of community identification. This is a universal competence contradicted by its scattered achievements, a universal ability contradicted by its fragmented, scattered and disorganized execution. Hence, the speculations at the level of myth to begin with, then at the level of the philosophy of language when it ponders the origin of the scattering-confounding. In this respect, the myth of Babel, too short and too confused in its literary construction, lets us imagine, in a regressive movement, a supposed lost paradisiacal language; it does not include a guide to behaving in this labyrinth. The scattering-confounding is then perceived as an irremediable linguistic catastrophe. In a moment, I will suggest a more benign reading with regard to the normal condition of human beings.

But to begin with, I want to say that there is a second fact which must not obscure the first, that of the diversity of languages: the equally well-known fact that people have always translated; before the professional interpreters, there were the travellers, the merchants, the ambassadors, the spies, and that makes for a lot of bilinguals and polyglots! Here we are broaching a feature as remarkable as the lamented incommunicability, namely, the very fact of translation, which presupposes that every speaker has the ability to learn and to use languages other than his own: this capacity appears firmly attached to other more hidden features concerning the practical experience of language, features that will lead us at the end of our journey into the vicinity of intralinguistic translation processes, namely and to anticipate, the reflexive capacity of language, that possibility, always on hand, of speaking on the subject of language, of placing it at a distance, and in this way of treating our own language as one language among others. I shall keep this analysis of the reflexivity of language for later and concentrate on the simple fact of translation. Men speak different languages, but they can learn others besides their native language.

This simple fact has given rise to huge speculation, which has let itself become locked into ruinous alternatives from which it must extricate itself. These paralysing alternatives are the following: either the diversity of languages gives expression to a radical heterogeneity – and in that case translation is theoretically impossible; one language is untranslatable *a priori* into another. Or else, taken as a fact, translation is explained by a common fund that renders the fact of translation possible; but then we must be able either to find this common fund, and this is the *original* language track, or to reconstruct it logically, and this is the *universal* language track; original or

The paradigm of translation

13

universal, this absolute language has to be such that it can be shown, with its phonological, lexical, syntactic and rhetorical inventories. I repeat the theoretical alternatives: either the diversity of languages is radical, and then translation is impossible by right, or else translation is a fact, and we must establish its rightful possibility through an inquiry into the origin or through a reconstruction of the *a priori* conditions of the noted fact.

I suggest that we need to get beyond these theoretical alternatives, translatable *versus* untranslatable, and to replace them with new practical alternatives, stemming from the very exercise of translation, the faithfulness *versus* betrayal alternatives, even if it means admitting that the practice of translation remains a risky operation which is always in search of its theory. At the end, we will see that the difficulties of intralinguistic translation confirm this embarrassing admission: I recently took part in an international colloquium on interpretation where I heard the talk given by the analytic philosopher Donald Davidson, entitled: 'Theoretically Difficult, Hard and Practically Simple, Easy'.

This is also my thesis as regards the two sides of translation, extra- and intralinguistic: theoretically incomprehensible, but actually practicable, for the huge price that we are about to name; the practical alternatives of faithfulness *versus* betrayal.

Before getting onto the path of this practical dialectic, faithfulness *versus* betrayal, I should like to state very suc-cinctly the reasons for the speculative impasse where the untranslatable and the translatable jostle together.

The thesis of the untranslatable is the necessary conclusion of a certain ethnolinguistics – B. Lee Whorf, E. Sapir – which endeavoured to underline the non-superimposable character of the different divisions on which the numerous linguistic systems rest: the phonetic and articulatory division at the root of the phonological systems (vowels, consonants, etc.), the conceptual division commanding the lexical systems (dictionaries, encyclopaedias, etc.), the syntactic division at the root of the various grammars. The examples abound: if you say 'wood' [bois] in French, you put ligneous materials and the idea of a little forest together; but in another language, these two meanings will not be connected and will be reassembled in two different semantic systems; on the grammatical plane, it is easy to see that the systems of verb tenses (present, past, future) differ from one language to another; you have languages where the position in time is not marked, but rather the performed or non-performed character of the action: and you have languages without verb tenses where the position in time is marked only by adverbs equivalent to 'yesterday', 'tomorrow', etc. If you add the idea that each linguistic division imposes a worldview, an idea that to my way of thinking is untenable, saying for example that the Greeks constructed ontologies because they have a verb 'to be' which functions both as a copula and as an affirmation of existence, then it is the set of human relationships of the speakers of a given language that turns out to be non-superimposable on the set of such relationships through which the speaker of another language is himself understood as he understands his relationship to the world. So we must conclude that misunderstanding is a right, that translation is theoretically impossible and that bilinguals have to be schizophrenics.

In that case, we are thrown back onto the other bank: since there is such a thing as translation, it certainly has to be possible. And if it is possible, it means that, beneath the diversity of languages, there are hidden structures that *either* bear the trace of a lost original language that we must rediscover *or* consist of *a priori* codes, of universal structures or, as we say, transcendentals that we must manage to reconstruct. The first version – that of the original language – was professed by various Gnostics, by the Kabbala, by hermetisms of all kinds, even yielding some poisonous fruit like the plea for a supposed Aryan language, declared historically fecund, which they contrast with the supposed infertile Hebrew; in his book *The Languages of Paradise*, with the disquieting subtitle, 'Aryans and Semites: a providential pair', Olender denounces the perfidious linguistic anti-Semitism in what he terms, this 'clever yarn'; but, to be fair, we must say that the nostalgia for the original language has also produced the powerful meditation of a Walter Benjamin writing *The Translator's Task* where the 'perfect language', the 'pure language' – these are the author's expressions – appears as the messianic horizon of the act of translating, secretly ensuring the convergence of the idioms as they are taken to the pinnacle of poetic creativity. Unfortunately, the practice of translation does not receive any help from this nostalgia, remodelled as an eschatological waiting, and we may soon have to mourn the loss of the wish for perfection in order to take on the 'translator's task' without intoxication and in all sobriety.

The other version of the quest for unity is more hard-headed, not about an origin in time, but about the *a priori* codes; Umberto Eco devoted some useful chapters to these endeavours in his book *The Search for the Perfect Language* (*The Making of Europe*). As the philosopher Bacon stresses, it is a matter of eliminating the imperfections of the natural languages which are sources of what he calls the 'idols' of language. Leibniz will give substance to this requirement with his idea of the universal characteristic, which does not aim at anything less than drawing up a universal lexicon of simple ideas, complemented by a compilation of all the rules of composition among these veritable atoms of thought.

Well! We must go from there to the question of confidence – and that will be the turning point in our meditation; we must ask ourselves why this attempt fails and has to fail.

There are, of course, partial successes as regards Chomskyan generational grammars, but there is a complete failure on the lexical and the phonological side. And why? Because it is not the imperfections of the natural languages, but their very functioning that is an anathema. Simplifying to a degree what is a highly technical discussion, let us note two stumbling blocks: first, there is no consensus on what would characterize a perfect language at the level of the lexicon of original ideas entering into composition; this consensus presupposes a total equivalence between the sign and the thing, without anything arbitrary, thus more broadly between language and the world, something which constitutes either a tautology, a preferred division being decreed a picture of the world, or an unverifiable claim, in the absence of an exhaustive survey of all the spoken languages. The second, even more fearsome, stumbling block is: no one can say how the natural languages, with all the peculiarities which we will talk about later, could be derived from the supposed perfect language: the *gap* between the universal and empirical languages, between what is *a priori* and what is historical, certainly appears insurmountable. It is here that our closing remarks on the work of translation within a selfsame natural language will certainly be useful in bringing to light the infinite complexities of those languages which make it necessary each time to learn the functioning of a language, including one's own. Such is the basic assessment of the dispute which brings together the relativism of the terrain, which must conclude that translation is impossible, and the closet formalism, which fails to found the fact of translation on a demonstrable universal structure. Yes, we must confess: from one language to another, the situation is definitely that of scattering and confounding. And *yet* translation is inscribed in the long litany of 'despite everything'. Despite fratricides, we campaign for universal fraternity. Despite the heterogeneity of idioms, there are bilinguals, polyglots, interpreters and translators.

SO, HOW DO THEY DO IT?

I just announced a change in direction: leaving the speculative alternatives — translatability against untranslatability — let us, I said, get to the practical alternatives — faithfulness against betrayal.

To put us on the right track for this change in direction, I should like to go back over the interpretation of the myth of Babel, which I would not like to conclude with the idea of a linguistic catastrophe inflicted on humans by a god who is jealous of their success. It is also possible to read this myth, as well as all the other commencement myths, I may add, which take irreversible situations into account, as the non-judgemental acknowledgement of an original separation. We can begin, early in Genesis, with the separation of cosmic elements which allows an order to emerge from chaos; we can continue with the loss of innocence and the expulsion from the Garden which also denotes entry into responsible adulthood, and then we can go — and we are terribly interested in this as a rereading of the myth of Babel — through the fratricide, the murder of Abel, which makes fraternity itself an ethical project and not a simple fact of nature. If one takes up this line of reading, which I share with the exegete Paul Beauchamp, the scattering and the confounding of languages, announced by the myth of Babel, are going to crown this history of the separation when they bring it to the heart of the exercise of language. This is how we are, this is how we exist, scattered and confounded, and called to what? Well . . . to translation! There is a post-Babel, defined by 'the translator's task', to take up again the already mentioned title of Walter Benjamin's famous essay.

To give more weight to this reading, I will recall with Umberto Eco that the narrative in Genesis 11, 1–9 is preceded by two verses numbered Genesis 10, 31–32, where the plurality of languages seems to be taken for a merely factual datum. I read these verses in Chouraki's rough translation:[3]

These are the sons of Shem, after their families, after their tongues, in their lands, after their nations.

These are the families of the sons of Noah, after their generations, in their nations: and by these were the nations divided in the earth after the flood.

These verses are similar in form to a census, where the simple curiosity of a benevolent glance expresses itself. Translation is definitely a task, then, not in the sense of a restricting obligation, but in the sense of the thing to be done so that human action can simply continue, to speak like Benjamin's friend Hannah Arendt, in The Human Condition.

The narrative entitled 'The Myth of Babel' follows, then:

And the whole earth was of one language, and of one speech.

And it came to pass, as they journeyed from the east, that they found a plain in the land of Shinar; and they dwelt there.

And they said one to another, Go to, let us make brick, and burn them throughly.

And they had brick for stone, and slime had they for mortar.

And they said, Go to, let us build us a city and a tower, whose top [may reach] unto heaven; and let us make us a name, lest we be scattered abroad upon the face of the whole earth.

And the LORD came down to see the city and the tower, which the children of men builded [*sic*].

And the LORD said, Behold, the people [is] one, and they have all one language; and this they begin to do: and now nothing will be restrained from them, which they have imagined to do.

Go to, let us go down, and there confound their language, that they may not understand one another's speech.

So the LORD scattered them abroad from thence upon the face of all the earth: and they left off to build the city.

Therefore is the name of it called Babel: because the LORD did there confound the language of all the earth: and from thence did the LORD scatter them abroad upon the face of all the earth.

These [are] the generations of Shem: Shem [was] an hundred years old, and begat Arphaxad two years after the flood:

And Shem lived after he begat Arphaxad five hundred years, and begat sons and daughters.[4]

You heard: there is no recrimination, no lamentation, no accusation: 'So the LORD scattered them abroad from thence upon the face of all the earth: and they left off to build the city.' They left off building the city! That is a way of saying: this is the way things are. Well, well! This is the way things are, as Benjamin liked to say. Starting from this fact of life, let us translate!

To speak accurately about the task of translating, I would

like to mention, following Antoine Berman in *The Test of the Foreign*, the *desire* to translate. This desire goes beyond constraint and usefulness. There is certainly a constraint: if we want to trade,[5] to travel, to negotiate, indeed to spy we definitely have to have messengers who speak the language of others. As for usefulness, it is patently obvious. If we want to save ourselves the bother of learning foreign languages, we will be very pleased to come across translations. After all, this is how we have had access to the tragic writers, to Plato, to Shakespeare, Cervantes, Petrarch and Dante, Goethe and Schiller, Tolstoy and Dostoyevsky. Constraint, usefulness, so be it! But more tenacious, more profound, more hidden than that there is: the desire to translate.

It is this desire that has driven the German thinkers since Goethe, the great classicist, and von Humboldt, whom I have already mentioned, through the Romantics, Novalis, the Schlegel brothers, Schleiermacher (the translator of Plato, we must not forget that), even Hölderlin, the tragic translator of Sophocles, and finally Walter Benjamin, Hölderlin's heir. And at the stern of this fine crew, Luther, the translator of the Bible – Luther and his will to 'germanize' the Bible, held captive by St Jerome's Latin.

What did these people with a passion for translation expect from their desire? What one of them called the *broadening* of the horizon of their own language – together with what they have all called formation, *Bildung*, that is to say, both configuration and education, and as a bonus, if I may put it that way, the discovery of their own language and of its resources which have been left to lie fallow. The following line is Hölderlin's: 'What is one's own must be learned as well as what is foreign.' For goodness' sake, why does this desire to translate have to be fobbed off with the prize of a dilemma, the *faithfulness/betrayal* dilemma? Because there is no absolute criterion for good translation; for such a criterion to be available, we would have to be able to compare the source and target texts with a third text which would bear the identical meaning that is supposed to be passed from the first to the second. The same thing said on both sides. As was the case for the Plato of the *Parmenides*, there is no third man between the idea of man and such-and-such a specific man – Socrates, so as not to name him! – nor is there a third text between the source text and the target text. Hence the paradox, before the dilemma: a good translation can aim only at a supposed *equivalence* that is not founded on a demonstrable *identity* of meaning. An equivalence without identity. This equivalence can only be sought, worked at, supposed. And the only way of criticizing a translation – something we can always do – is to suggest another supposed, alleged, better or different one. And this, moreover, is what happens in the world of professional translators. As far as the great texts of our culture are concerned, we essentially live on a few retranslations which are reworked over and over again. This is what happens with the Bible, with Homer, with Shakespeare, with all the writers cited above and with the philosophers, from Plato to Nietzsche and Heidegger.

Thus barded with retranslations, are we better armed for solving the faithfulness/betrayal dilemma? Not at all. The risk which the desire to translate is owed [*se paie*], and which transforms the encounter with the foreign in its language into a test, is insuperable. Franz Rosenzweig, whom our colleague Hans-Christoph Askani took as 'a witness to the problem of translation' (this is how I venture to translate the title of his great Tübingen book), gave this test the form of a paradox: to translate, he says, is to serve two masters, the foreigner in his strangeness, the reader in his desire for appropriation. Before him, Schleiermacher broke the paradox up into two phrases: 'bringing the reader to the author', 'bringing the author to the reader'. For my part, I venture to apply the Freudian vocabulary to that situation and to talk, not only about the work of translation, but also about the work of recollection and the work of mourning, as Freud does.

The work of translation, won on the battlefield of a secret resistance motivated by fear, indeed by hatred of the foreign, perceived as a threat against our own linguistic identity. But the work of mourning too, applied to renouncing the very ideal of the *perfect translation*. Indeed, this ideal has not only nurtured the desire to translate and, occasionally, the happiness of translating, it has also brought sorrow to a Hölderlin, broken by his ambition to found German and Greek poetry on a hyper-poetry where the difference in idioms would be abolished. And who knows whether it is not the ideal of the perfect translation which definitively maintains the nostalgia for the original language or the will for control over language by means of the universal language? Giving up the dream of the perfect translation is still the acknowledgement of the impassable difference between the peculiar and the foreign. It is still the test of the foreign.

It is here that I return to my title: the paradigm of translation.

Indeed, it seems to me that translation sets us not only intellectual work, theoretical or practical, but also an ethical problem. Bringing the reader to the author, bringing the author to the reader, at the risk of serving and of betraying two masters: this is to practise what I like to call *linguistic hospitality*. It is this which serves as a model for other forms of hospitality that I think resemble it: confessions, religions, are they not like languages that are foreign to one another, with their lexicon, their grammar, their rhetoric, their stylistics which we must learn in order to make our way into them? And is eucharistic hospitality not to be taken up with the same risks of translation-betrayal, but also with the same renunciation of the perfect translation? I retain these risky analogies and these question marks . . .

But I would not like to close without having said why we must not neglect the other half of the problem of translation, namely, if you remember it, translation within the same linguistic community. I would like to show, at least very succinctly, that it is in this same language's work on itself that underlying reasons for the insuperability of the gap between a supposed perfect universal language and the languages that we term natural, in the sense of non-artificial, are revealed. As I have suggested, it is not the imperfections of natural languages that we would like to do away with, but the very functioning of these languages in their astonishing peculiarities. And it is the work of internal translation that in fact reveals this gap. I come close here to the statement that commands the whole of George Steiner's book, *After Babel*. After Babel, 'to understand is to translate'. This is about much more than a simple internalization of the relationship to the foreign, in accordance with Plato's adage that thought is a dialogue of the soul with itself – an internalisation that would transform internal translation into a simple appendix to external translation. This is about an original investigation, which lays bare the everyday processes of a living language: these ensure that no universal language can succeed in reconstructing its indefinite diversity. This is really about approaching the mysteries of a language that is full of life, and at the same time, giving an account of the phenomenon of misunderstanding, of misinterpretation which, according to Schleiermacher, gives rise to interpretation, the theory of which hermeneutics wants to develop. The reasons for the gap between perfect language and a language that is full of life are exactly the same as the causes of misinterpretation.

I will start from this substantial fact, characteristic of the use of our languages: it is always possible *to say the same thing in another way*. This is what we do when we define one word using another word from the same lexicon, as all the dictionaries do. In his semiotic science, Peirce places this phenomenon at the centre of the reflexivity of language. But this is also what we do when we reformulate an argument which has not been understood. We say that we are explaining it, that is to say, that we are opening out the folds [*nous déployons les plis*]. Now, to say the same thing in another way − *in other words* − this is what a moment ago the foreign language translator did. Thus we rediscover, within our linguistic community, the same enigma of the same, of meaning itself, the identical meaning which cannot be found, and which is supposed to make the two versions of the same intention equivalent; this is why, as we say, we do not get out of it; and very often we make the misunderstanding worse with our explanations. At the same time, a bridge is thrown between internal translation, this is what I call it, and external translation, namely, that within the same community, understanding requires at least two interlocutors: these are not foreigners admittedly, but already others, other close relations, if you want: this is what Husserl, talking about the knowledge of others, calls the everyday other, *der Fremde*, the foreigner. There is something foreign in every other. It is as several people that we define, that we reformulate, that we explain, that we try to say *the same thing in another way*.

Let us take another step towards those great mysteries that Steiner never ceases to visit and revisit. With what do we work when we speak and address an other?

With three kinds of units: *words*, that is to say, signs that we find in the lexicon, *sentences*, for which there is no lexicon (no one can say how many sentences have been and will be uttered in French or in any other language), and finally *texts*, that is to say, sequences of sentences. It is the handling of these three kinds of units, one checked off by Saussure, another by Benveniste and Jacobson, the third by Harald Weinrich, Jauss and the text reception theorists, that is the source of the gap in relation to a supposed perfect language, and the source of the misunderstanding in everyday usage and, as such, the occasion for multiple and competing interpretations.

Two words on the word: each of our words has more than one meaning, as we see in the dictionaries. We call that *polysemy*. The meaning is thus defined each time through usage, which basically consists in screening the part of the word's meaning which suits the rest of the sentence and with it contributes to the unity of meaning expressed and offered for exchange. It is the context each time which, as we say, determines the meaning that the word has acquired in such-and-such a circumstance of discourse: from then on, the arguments over words can be endless: What did you mean? etc. And it is in the play of the question and the answer that things become clearer or become confused. For there are not only obvious contexts, there are hidden contexts and what we call the *connotations* which are not all intellectual, but affective, not all public, but peculiar to a circle, to a class, a group, or perhaps even a secret society; there is thus the whole margin hidden by censorship, prohibition, the margin of what is unspoken, criss-crossed by all the figures of the hidden.

With this recourse to the context, we have gone from the word to the sentence. This new unit, which is in fact the first unit of discourse, the word falling within the domain of the sign unit which is not yet discourse, brings with it new sources of ambiguity chiefly concerning the relationship of the signified – what we say – to the referent – that about which we speak, ultimately the world. A vast programme, as they say! Now, for want of a full description, we only have points of view, perspectives, partial visions of the world. That is why we have never ceased making ourselves clear, making ourselves clear with words and sentences, making ourselves clear to others who do not see things from the same angle as we do.

So, the texts come into play, these sequences of sentences which, as the word indicates, are *textures* which *weave* the discourse into longer or shorter sequences. Narrative is one of the most remarkable of these sequences, and is particularly interesting for our talk insofar as we learned that we can always tell a story in another way by changing the plot, the fable. But there are also all of the other kinds of texts, where one does something other than narrate, for example arguing, as we do in moral philosophy, in law, in politics. Rhetoric plays a part here with its stylistic devices, its tropes, metaphor and others, and all the language games in the service of countless strategies, among them seduction and intimidation at the expense of the honourable concern with persuasion.

All that we were able to say in translation studies about the complicated relations between thought and language, about the spirit and the letter, and about the eternal question as to whether we should translate the meaning or translate the words follows from this. All these problems associated with translation from one language to another find their origin in language's reflection on itself, which made Steiner say that 'to understand is to translate'.

But I shall turn to what Steiner is most fond of and what could easily tip the whole talk over in a direction contrary to that of the test of the foreign. Steiner enjoys investigating the uses of speech where one aims at something other than the true, other than the real, that is to say, not only the false declaration, namely, the lie — although to speak is to be able to lie, to conceal, to falsify — but also all that we can classify in terms of something other than the real: let us say, the possible, the conditional, the optative, the hypothetical, the utopian. It is *incredible* — you've said it! — what we can do with language: not only can we say the same thing *in another way*, but we can say something *other* than what is the case. On this subject — and with what confusion! — Plato mentioned the figure of the Sophist.

But it is not this figure that has the greatest capacity to change the nature of our talk: it is language's propensity for the enigma, for artifice, for abstruseness, for the secret, in fact for non-communication. Hence, what I will call Steiner's extremism which leads him, through hatred of chattering, of conventional usage, of the instumentalization of language, to contrast interpretation with communication; the equation 'To understand is to translate' closes, then, on the one to oneself relationship in the *secret* where we rediscover the untranslatable, which we had thought we had moved away from in favour of the faithfulness/betrayal pair. We rediscover it on the vow of the utmost faithfulness route. But faithfulness to whom and to what? Faithfulness to language's capacity for safeguarding the secret contrary to its proclivity to betray it; consequently, faithfulness to itself rather than to others. And it is true that the glorious poetry of a Paul Celan is bordering on the untranslatable, bordering at first on the unspeakable, the loathsome, at the heart of his own language as well as in the gap between two languages.

What are we to conclude from this series of reversals? I confess that I am still perplexed. I am inclined to favour entry through the foreign door, that is for sure. Have we not been set in motion by the fact of human plurality and by the double enigma of incommunicability between idioms and of translation in spite of everything? And then, without the test of the foreign, would we be sensitive to the strangeness of our own language? Finally, without that test, would we not be in danger of shutting ourselves away in the sourness of a monologue, alone with our books? Credit, then, to linguistic hospitality.

But I see the other side perfectly well too, that of language's work on itself. Is it not this work which gives us the key to the difficulties of translation *ad extra*? And if we had not skirted the disquieting regions of the unspeakable, would we have the sense of the secret, of the untranslatable secret? And our better exchanges, in love and in friendship, would they save this quality of discretion – secret/discretion – which safeguards the distance in the proximity?

Yes, there really are two routes of entry into the problem of translation.

Three

For Jean Greisch

My contribution focuses on the paradox that is both at the origin of translation and an effect of translation, i.e. the characteristic of a spoken message that is in a sense untranslatable from one language to another.

1. There is a first untranslatable, an initial untranslatable, which is the multiplicity of languages. It would be better immediately to call it, as von Humboldt does, the *diversity*, the dissimilarity of languages, suggesting the idea of a radical heterogeneity that should render translation impossible *a priori*. This diversity affects all the operating levels of language: the phonetic and articulatory division at the root of phonetic systems; the lexical division that separates languages, not word for word, but from lexical system to lexical system, verbal meanings within a lexicon consisting in a network of differences and of synonyms; the syntactic division affecting, for example, the verbal systems and the position of an event in time or even the modes of linking and of consecution. That is not all; languages are different not only owing to the way they carve up reality but also owing to the way they put it together again at the level of discourse; in this respect Benveniste, replying to Saussure, observes that the basic unit

of meaningful language is the sentence and not the word whose oppositive character we have recalled. Now the sentence organizes in a synthetic way a speaker, an interlocutor, a message that tries to signify something and a referent, i.e. that about which one speaks, that of which one speaks (someone says something to someone about something in accordance with the rules of significance [*signifiance*]). It is at this level that the untranslatable proves disquieting a second time; not only the carving up of reality, but the relationship of sense to referent; what one says in its relationship to that about which one says it; throughout the world sentences flutter between men like elusive butterflies. That is not all, nor is it even the most fearsome issue; sentences are short discourses taken from longer discourses known as texts. Translators know it perfectly well: it is texts, not sentences, not words, that our texts try to translate. And texts in turn are part of cultural groups through which different visions of the world are expressed, visions which moreover can confront each other within the same elementary system of phonological, lexical, syntactic division, to the extent of making what one calls the national or the community culture a network of visions of the world in secret or open competition. Let us think only about the West and its successive contributions, Greek, Latin, Hebrew, and about its periods of competitive self-understanding, from the Middle Ages to the Renaissance and the Reformation, to the Enlightenment, to Romanticism.

These considerations lead me to say that the work of the translator does not move from the word to the sentence, to the text, to the cultural group, but conversely: absorbing vast interpretations of the spirit of a culture, the translator comes down again from the text, to the sentence and to the word. The final act, if one can put it that way, the final decision is about making out a glossary at the level of words: the selection of the glossary is the final test where what should be impossible to translate is crystallized as it were in fine.

2. I have just spoken about the initial untranslatable. In order to reach the final untranslatable, the one translation produces, it is necessary to say how translation works, because *there is translation*. We have always translated: there always were the merchants, the travellers, the ambassadors, the spies to satisfy the need to extend human exchanges beyond the linguistic community, which is one of the essential components of social cohesion and of group identity. Men of one culture have always known that there were foreigners who had different customs and different languages. And the foreigner has always been disturbing: so there were other ways of life than our own were there? Translation always was a partial response to this 'test of the foreign'. It presupposes a curiosity initially – how, asks the eighteenth-century rationalist, can one be Persian? We know Montesquieu's paradoxes: imagine the Persian interpretation of the customs of Western, Greco-Latin, Christian, superstitious and rationalist man. What Antoine Berman, in *The Test of the Foreign*, calls the *desire to translate* is grafted onto this curiosity about the foreigner.

How does the translator do it? I am deliberately using the verb 'to do' because it is through a doing, in pursuit of its theory, that the translator gets over the obstacle – and even the theoretical objection – of the impossibility of mechanically reproducing something in another language. In an earlier essay, I recall the attempts to provide a theoretical solution to this dilemma of the mechanical impossibility and the practice of translation: either the recourse to an original language or the venture of constructing an artificial language, which Umberto Eco rediscovered in *The Search for the Perfect Language* (*The Making of*

Europe). I am not going back to the arguments which consume the failure of these two attempts: the arbitrariness of the reconstruction of the original language, which ultimately seems nowhere to be found. Perhaps it is even a pure fantasy: the fantasy of the origin rendered historical, the desperate refusal of the real human condition, which is that of multiplicity at all the levels of existence, multiplicity, whose most disquieting expression is the diversity of languages: why so many languages? Answer: this is the way things are. We are, by constitution and not by chance, which would be a fault, 'After Babel', according to Steiner's title. As regards the perfect language as artificial language, besides the fact that no one has succeeded in writing it down, the difference between the supposed artificial language and the natural languages with their idiosyncrasy, their peculiarities, proves to be insurmountable, as there is no fulfilment of the preliminary condition of an exhaustive enumeration of simple ideas and of a unique universal procedure of derivation. Let us add to this difference a further difference in the way the various languages deal with the relationship between sense and reference, in the relationship between expressing the real, expressing something other than the real, the possible, the unreal, the utopian idea, indeed even the secret, the inexpressible, in short the other of what can be communicated. Every language's struggle with the secret, the hidden, the mystery, the inexpressible is above all else the most entrenched incommunicable, initial untranslatable.

So how do they do it? In my earlier essay, I tried a handy way out, substituting for the paralysing alternatives – translatable *versus* untranslatable – the alternatives faithfulness *versus* betrayal, even if it did mean admitting that the practice of translation remains a risky operation which is always in search of its theory.

I would like to go back over this admission, accentuating what I call the final untranslatable revealed, and even produced, by translation. The faithfulness/betrayal dilemma claims to be a practical dilemma because there is no absolute criterion of what would count as good translation. This absolute criterion would be *the same meaning*, written somewhere, on top of and between the original text and the target text. This third text would be the bearer of the identical meaning, supposed to move from the first to the second. Hence, the paradox, concealed behind the practical dilemma between faithfulness and betrayal: a good translation can aim only at a supposed equivalence, not founded on a demonstrable identity of meaning, equivalence without identity. We, then, can link this supposition of equivalence without identity with the *work* of translation, which shows itself most clearly in the phenomenon of retranslation which one observes at the level of humanity's great texts, in particular those which get over the barrier of the disparity in the systems of division and of phrasal and word for word reconstruction mentioned above, for example between the Hebrew, the Greek and the Latin, or between Chinese and the languages of India. Nor do we stop retranslating within the same cultural zone, as we see with the Bible, Homer, Shakespeare and Dostoyevsky. This work is reassuring for the reader, because it allows him to access works of a foreign culture whose language he does not speak. But what about the translator and his faithfulness/betrayal dilemma? The great *desirers* of translation who were the German Romantics, whose venture Antoine Berman recounts in *The Test of the Foreign*, multiplied the versions of this practical dilemma that they dispelled in phrases like: 'bringing the reader to the author', 'bringing the author to the reader'. What they dispelled was the anguish of serving two masters, the foreigner in his strangeness, the reader in his desire for appropriation. We would contribute towards this dispelling by suggesting the abandonment of the dream of the perfect translation and by admitting to the total difference between the peculiar and the foreign. I would like to renew this admission here.

Even so, what has been presupposed, under the seemingly unpretentious phrase of equivalence without identity, is the prior existence of this *meaning* that the translation is supposed to 'render', as we say, with the muddled idea of a 'restitution'. This equivalence can only be sought, worked at, supposed.

It is this presupposition that must be challenged. It is relatively acceptable within a vast cultural area where the community identities, including linguistic, are themselves the product of long-lasting exchanges, as is the case in the Indo-European area, and all the more so in the affinity sub-groups like the Romance languages, the Germanic languages and the Slavonic languages, and in dual relationships as between a Latin language and a Germanic language, say Anglo-Saxon. So the presupposition of equivalence seems acceptable. In actual fact, the cultural kinship hides the true nature of equivalence, which is *produced* by translation rather than *presupposed* by it. I am referring to a work that is not directly linked to translation, but which sheds light in a lateral way on the phenomenon that I am trying to describe: the production of equivalence through translation. The book is by Marcel Détienne (a Hellenic scholar) and is entitled *Comparing the Incomparable* [*Comparer l'incomparable*].[1] It is levelled against the slogan: 'We can only compare the comparable' (pp. 45–6), so he talks about 'constructive comparative studies'. Where Antoine Berman talked about 'the test of the foreign', Détienne talks about the 'shock of the incomparable'. The incomparable, he observes, confronts us with 'the strangeness of first words and first beginnings' (p. 48).

Let us apply the following formula to translation: 'constructing comparables'. I found an illustration of the application of this formula in the interpretation that a brilliant French sinologist, François Jullien, gives of the relationship between ancient China and ancient and classical Greece. His thesis, which I do not dispute, but which I take as a working hypothesis, is that Chinese is the absolute other of Greek — that knowledge of the inside of Chinese amounts to a deconstruction of what is outside, of what is exterior, i.e. thinking and speaking Greek. So the absolute strangeness is on our side, it belongs to we who think and speak Greek, whether it is in German or in a Latin language. Pushed to the extreme, the thesis is that Chinese and Greek can be distinguished by an initial 'fold' [pli] in what can be thought and what can be experienced, a 'fold' beyond which we cannot go. Thus, in his last book, entitled Du temps [Of Time],[2] Jullien maintains that Chinese verbs do not have tenses because Chinese does not have the concept of time worked out by Aristotle in Physics IV, then reconstructed by Kant in 'The Transcendental Aesthetic', and finally universalized by Hegel through the ideas of the negative and the Aufhebung. Hegel's whole book takes the form: 'there is not . . . there is not . . . but there is'. So I raise the question: how do we speak (in French) about what there is in Chinese? Now Jullien does not utter a word of Chinese in his book (apart from yin-yang!); he speaks in French, in a beautiful language I may add, about what there is in place of time, i.e. the seasons, occasions, roots and leaves, springs and incoming tides. By doing this, he constructs comparables. And he constructs them downwards, as I mentioned above with reference to what one does while translating, i.e. from the general intuition concerning the difference in the 'fold', passing through the works, the Chinese classics, and then going down towards the words. In the end the construction of the comparable expresses itself in the construction of a glossary. And what do we find concerning the words of our 'Greek' languages? Ordinary words that have not had a philosophical destiny and which, owing to the effect of translation, are removed from contexts of use and promoted to the rank of *equivalents*, those great equivalents without identity, whose antecedent reality we had presupposed, believing that it was hidden somewhere so to speak, and the translator would discover it.

Grandeur of translation, risk of translation: creative betrayal of the original, equally creative appropriation by the reception language; *construction of the comparable*.

But is that not what happened in several periods of our own culture, when the Seventy translated the Hebrew Bible into Greek, into what we call the Septuagint, something that Hebrew specialists alone can criticize at their leisure? And St Jerome did it again with the Vulgate, construction of a Latin comparable. But before Jerome the Latins had created comparables, by deciding for all of us that *aretē* was translated by *virtus*, *polis* by *urbs* and *politēs* by *civis*. To remain in the biblical domain, we could say that Luther not only constructed a comparable in translating the Bible into German, in 'germanizing' it, as he dared to say, in the face of St Jerome's Latin, but created the German language, as comparable to Latin, to the Greek of the Septuagint, and to the Hebrew of the Bible.

3. Have we followed the idea of the untranslatable through to its logical conclusion? No, since we solved the mystery of equivalence by constructing it. The construction of the

comparable has even become the justification for a double betrayal insofar as the two incommensurable masters were rendered commensurable through the translation-construction. So there remains a final untranslatable that we discover through the construction of the comparable. That construction is accomplished at the level of 'meaning', the only word that we have not commented on, because we took it for granted. Now the *meaning* is extracted from the unity it shares with the flesh of words, that flesh which we call the 'letter'. Translators gladly removed it, so as not to be accused of 'literal translation'; translating literally, is that not translating word for word? What shame! What disgrace! Now excellent translators, modelled on Hölderlin, on Paul Celan and, in the biblical domain, on Meschonnic, fought a campaign against the *isolated meaning*, the meaning without the letter, contrary to the letter. They gave up the comfortable shelter of the *equivalence of meaning*, and ventured into hazardous areas where there would be some talk of tone, of savour, of rhythm, of spacing, of silence between the words, of metrics and of rhyme. Undoubtedly, the vast majority of translators rush to oppose this, without recognizing that translating the isolated meaning means repudiating an achievement of contemporary semiotics, the unity of meaning and sound, of the signified and the signifier, in opposition to the prejudice one still finds in the early Husserl: that the meaning is complete in the act of 'conferring meaning', of *Sinngebung*. Husserl treats expression (*Ausdruck*) like an article of clothing external to the body, which really is the incorporeal soul of meaning, of the *Bedeutung*. The result is that only a poet can translate a poet. But I would reply to Berman, were he still alive – dear Berman who, sadly, has left us and whom we miss – I would reply that he has moved the construction of the comparable a stage further, to the level of the letter; on the basis of the disquieting success of a Hölderlin who speaks Greek in German and, perhaps, on the basis of that of a Meschonnic, who speaks Hebrew in French . . . So the 'literal' translation, which he chases relentlessly, is not a word for word translation, but a letter for letter one. Did he go as far as he believed he had, in his nearly hopeless criticism of the equivalence of meaning to meaning, of the construction of a comparable, of a literal comparable? Is not the continuity in the struggle against the constantly recurring untranslatable read in the closeness of two successive titles: *The Test of the Foreign* and *Translation and the Letter or the Faraway Inn* [*La traduction et la lettre ou l'auberge du lointain*[3]].

Notes

Introduction

1 Paul Ricoeur, *Sur la traduction* (Paris: Bayard, 2004); translated here by Eileen Brennan as *On Translation*.

2 I am indebted to Dominico Jervolino for this reference to Dolar and to several other sources on the history of translation cited below. See his illuminating paper, 'The hermeneutics of the self and the paradigm of translation', presented at the Rome International Conference on Translation (April 2004) and his Introduction to *La traduzione: una sfida etuca* (Brescia: Morcelliana, 2001), pp. 7–35. See also his pioneering essay, 'Herméneutique et traduction. L'autre, l'étranger, l'hôte', *Archives de Philosophie* 63 (2000), pp. 79–93.

3 Antoine Berman, *L'épreuve de l'étranger* (Paris: Gallimard, 1984).

4 Jervolino, 'The hermeneutics of the self'. See also Paul Zumthor, *Babel ou l'inachèvement* (Paris: Seuil, 1997).

5 Émile Benveniste, *Le vocabulaire des institutions indo-européennes* (Paris: Minuit, 1969).

6 Ricoeur, *Sur la traduction*, pp. 19–20.

7 Jervolino, 'The hermeneutics of the self'; see also Jervolino, 'Translation as paradigm for hermeneutics and its implications for an ethics of hospitality', *Ars Interpretandi* 5 (2000), pp. 57–69.

8 Jervolino, 'The hermeneutics of the self' and 'La question de l'unité de l'œuvre de Ricoeur: la paradigme de la traduction', *Archives de Philosophie* 4 (2004), pp. 659–68.

9 Ricoeur, *La Mémoire, l'histoire, l'oubli* (Paris: Seuil, 2001), p. 657; English translation by David Pellauer, *Memory, History and Forgetting* (Chicago: University of Chicago Press, 2005).

Translation as challenge and source of happiness

1 *Deutsches Verlagsanstalt*. It is both a branch of the Bosch Foundation and a publishing house.

2 Antoine Berman, *L'épreuve de l'étranger* (Paris: Gallimard, 1984, 1995). [S. Heyvaert translated this book into English under the title, *The Experience of the Foreign: Culture and Translation in Romantic Germany* (New York: SUNY Press, 1992). However, for reasons to do with Ricoeur's subsequent reflections on the meaning of the word *épreuve*, I am unable to fully adopt Heyvaert's rendition of Berman's title. EB.]

The paradigm of translation

1 George Steiner, *After Babel: Aspects of Language and Translation* (Oxford: Oxford Paperbacks, 1998).

2 The words, 'signs which . . . concern things' render the French *signes qui . . . valent pour des choses*, but the English verb 'concern' does not capture a possible connotation of the French verb *valoir*. In this context, *valoir* also carries the associated sense of 'being worth something', an association that Ricoeur draws upon when he goes on to talk about 'the exchange of signs in interlocution'. EB

3 This is certainly one of those occasions when, reading Ricoeur in English, we have to accept that something has been lost in translation. Thus, losing all sense of the roughness of Chouraki's French rendition of the Hebrew Bible, we hear instead the lyrical cadences of the King James version. EB

4 This again is the King James version.

5 The original French text reads as follows: *si on veut commencer, voyager, négocier, voire espionner il faut bien disposer de messagers qui parlent la langue des autres*. As the word *commencer*, meaning 'to begin', makes little sense in this context, I assume that this is a typesetting error and that the correct word is *commercer*, meaning 'to trade'. EB

A 'passage': translating the untranslatable

1 Marcel Détienne, *Comparer l'incomparable* (Paris: Seuil, 2000).

2 François Jullien, *Du temps*, Paris: Grasset et Fasquelle, 2001.

3 A. Berman, *La traduction et la lettre ou l'auberge du lointain* (Paris: Seuil, 1999).

Index

THINKING IN ACTION

…Big ideas to fit in your pocket

Title	Author	Pb ISBN	Pb ISBN-13	Price UK	Price US
On Translation	Paul Ricoeur	0415357780	9780415357784	£9.99	$17.95
On Education	Harry Brighouse	0415327903	9780415327909	£9.99	$17.95
On the Human Condition	Dominique Janicaud	0415327962	9780415327961	£9.99	$17.95
On the Public	Alastair Hannay	0415327938	9780415327930	£9.99	$17.95
On the Political	Chantal Mouffe	0415305217	9780415305211	£9.99	$17.95
On Belief	Slavoj Zizek	0415255325	9780415255325	£9.99	$17.95
On Cosmopolitanism and Forgiveness	Jacques Derrida	0415227127	9780415227129	£9.99	$17.95
On Film	Stephen Mulhall	0415247969	9780415247962	£9.99	$17.95
On Being Authentic	Charles Guignon	0415261236	9780415261234	£9.99	$17.95
On Humour	Simon Critchley	0415251214	9780415251211	£9.99	$17.95
On Immigration and Refugees	Sir Michael Dummett	0415227089	9780415227087	£9.99	$17.95
On Anxiety	Reneta Salecl	0415312760	9780415312769	£9.99	$17.95
On Literature	Hillis Miller	0415261252	9780415261258	£9.99	$17.95
On Religion	John D Caputo	041523333X	9780415233330	£9.99	$17.95
On Humanism	Richard Norman	0415305233	9780415305238	£9.99	$17.95
On Science	Brian Ridley	0415249805	9780415249805	£9.99	$17.95
On Stories	Richard Kearney	0415247985	9780415247986	£9.99	$17.95
On Personality	Peter Goldie	0415305144	9780415305143	£9.99	$17.95
On the Internet	Hubert Dreyfus	0415228077	9780415228077	£9.99	$17.95
On Evil	Adam Morton	0415305195	9780415305198	£9.99	$17.95
On the Meaning of Life	John Cottingham	0415248000	9780415248006	£9.99	$17.95
On Cloning	John Harris	0415317002	9780415317009	£9.99	$17.95

Available from all good bookshops
Or buy online at: www.routledge.com

Related titles from Routledge

On Evil
Adam Morton

'This essay elucidates a picture of those who commit "evil" acts as lacking a mental "barrier" to stop them, using examples from recent history and pop-culture treatments from Buffy to Hannibal Lecter' – *Steven Poole, The Guardian*

'The author actually does what too few academics do: exhibit thought in action, not substituting the stale cite for an original idea.' – *Fred Alford, author of What Evil Means to Us*

Evil has long fascinated psychologists, philosophers, novelists and playwrights but remains an incredibly difficult concept to talk about.

On Evil is a compelling and at times disturbing tour of the many faces of evil. What is evil, and what makes people do awful things? If we can explain evil, do we explain it away? Can we imagine the mind of a serial killer, or does such evil defy description? Does evil depend on a contrast with good, as religion tells us, or can there be evil for evil's sake?

Adam Morton argues that any account of evil must help us understand three things: why evil occurs; why evil often arises out of banal or everyday situations; and how we can be seen as evil. Drawing on fascinating examples as diverse as *Augustine, Buffy the Vampire Slayer*, psychological studies of deviant behaviour and profiles of serial killers, Adam Morton argues that evil occurs when internal, mental barriers against it simply break down. He also introduces us to some nightmare people, such as Adolf Eichmann and Hannibal Lecter, reminding us that understanding their actions as humans brings us closer to understanding evil.

Exciting and thought–provoking, *On Evil* is essential reading for anyone interested in a topic that attracts and repels us in equal measure.

ISBN10: 0–415–30518–7 (hbk) ISBN10: 0–415–30519–5 (pbk)
ISBN13: 978–0–415–30518–1 (hbk) ISBN13: 978–0–415–30519–8 (pbk)

Available at all good bookshops
For ordering and further information please visit:
www.routledge.com

Related titles from Routledge

On Religion
John D. Caputo

'Intellectual without being overly academic...one cheers his vigor and relishes his insights into the paradoxical, ambiguous nature of religion and religious belief. Recommended.' – *Library Journal (USA)*

'With some deft sophistry (heavily influenced by Derrida who also produced one of the other five books in the Routledge's new Thinking in Action series) John D. Caputo redefines religion as love of the unforeseeable. And, as that is a given in life, his definition of religiosity pretty much equates with my definition of joie de vivre. So the opposite of a religious person is not an atheist, merely a "pusillanimous curmudgeon". But it's not all just clever wordplay. With his unorthodox definitions in place, Caputo goes on to denounce dogma, put Marx, Nietzsche and Freud in their historical places and to reunite religion, mysticism and science. On top of all that, there's a detailed deconstruction of religion in Star Wars. I'm converted.' – *Laurence Phelan, The Independent on Sunday*

'I feel obliged to warn readers that I loved this book. I loved its passion, loved its ideas, and the loved the alternately sassy and incantatory rhythms of its prose ... get this book and read it' – *Sea of Faith*

On Religion is a thrilling and accessible exploration of religious faith today. If God is dead, why is religion back? Digging up the roots of all things religious, John D. Caputo inspects them with clarity and style. Along the way, some fascinating questions crop up: What do I love when I love my God? What can the film *Star Wars* tell us about religion and what does 'may the force be with you' really mean? What are people doing when they perform an act 'in the name of God'?

ISBN10: 0–415–23332–1 (hbk)   ISBN10: 0–415–23333–x (pbk)
ISBN13: 978–0–415–23332–3 (hbk)   ISBN13: 978–0–415–23333–0 (pbk)

Available at all good bookshops
For ordering and further information please visit:
www.routledge.com

Related titles from Routledge

On the Meaning of Life
John Cottingham

'Cottingham summarises arguments about morality, evolution ... with clarity.'
– *Steven Poole, The Guardian*

'Elegantly written and accessible...Readers will appreciate Cottingham's clarity and his willingness to enter some difficult and complex areas of debate.' – *The Philosophers' Magazine*

'Lucid and provocative, rich with references and ideas...Cottingham takes things remarkably far for our day and age.'– *International Philosophical Quarterly*

'If Cottingham is brusque he can also be invigorating, and he focuses very effectively on the most fertile question in the so-called philosophy of life: that the "precariousness of human life and happiness" is exactly what makes our life interesting.' – *Jonathan Ree, Times Literary Supplement*

The question 'What is the meaning of life?' is one of the most fascinating, oldest and most difficult questions human beings have ever posed themselves. In an increasingly secularized culture, it remains a question to which we are ineluctably and powerfully drawn. In this acute and thoughtful book, John Cottingham assesses some of the most influential attempts to explain it, ranging from the bleak existentialist view to the religious demand that human beings amount to something more than Pascal's 'imbecile worms of the earth'. He asks what is involved in the 'disenchantment' of the natural world by science, and argues that, properly understood, modern cosmology and evolutionary theory need not foreclose the possibility of ultimate meaning. He also reflects on the paradox that the very impermanence and fragility of the human condition may lend support to the quest for a 'spiritual' dimension of meaning. Drawing skilfully on a wealth of thinkers, writers and scientists from Augustine, Descartes, Freud and Camus, to Spinoza, Pascal, Darwin, and Wittgenstein, *On the Meaning of Life* breathes new vitality into one of the very biggest questions.

ISBN10: 0–415–24799–3 (hbk)   ISBN10: 0–415–24800–0 (pbk)
ISBN13: 978–0–415–24799–3 (hbk)   ISBN13: 978–0–415–24800–6 (pbk)

Available at all good bookshops
For ordering and further information please visit:

www.routledge.com

Related titles from Routledge

On the Internet
Hubert L. Dreyfus

'A well-crafted polemic ... we need more teachers like Dreyfus himself, integrating the web into courses that are still deeply human.' – *Adam Morton, Times Literary Supplement*

'interesting and definitely much needed ... a short and thought provoking book that can be read by any net enthusiast and/or scholar who is interested in the topics of learning, knowledge and identity in relation to the Internet' – *Humanist*

Drawing on a diverse array of thinkers from Plato to Kierkegaard, *On the Internet* is one of the first books to bring philosophical insight to the debate on how far the internet can and cannot take us.

Dreyfus shows us the roots of the disembodied, free floating web surfer in Descartes' separation of mind and body, and how Kierkegaard's insights into the birth of the modern reading public anticipate the news-hungry, but disinterested risk avoiding internet junkie. Drawing on recent studies of the isolation experienced by many internet users, Dreyfus shows how the internet's privatization of experience ignores essential human capacities such as trust, moods, risk, shared local concerns and commitment. *On the Internet* is essential reading for anyone on line and all those interested in our place in the e-revolution.

ISBN10: 0–415–22806–9 (hbk)   ISBN10: 0–415–22807–7 (pbk)
ISBN13: 978–0–415–22806–0 (hbk)   ISBN13: 978–0–415–22807–7 (pbk)

Available at all good bookshops
For ordering and further information please visit:
www.routledge.com